MW01614997

THE STRUGGLE IS REAL
BUT SO IS GOD

ANDREW F CARTER

SHIFTED PRESS

This Devotional is dedicated to Kyra, for seeing the vision and pushing me to get it done. Thank you for the love, support and critical eye.

And to my sons, Andrew, Ezra and Zavier. Always keep your eyes on Him. I pray that you learn from my mistakes and are encouraged by my victories.

"Train up a child in the way he should go: and when he is old, he will not depart from it."

Proverbs 22:6 KJV

Introduction

God doesn't make mistakes. Every choice, every decision, every action has led you to this devotional for a specific purpose. God works with a purpose. Everything's a part of His plan and His will. Every sentence, every word and shared experience in this devotional was strategically placed by God because He knows you can take something from it. I've prayed over this devotional and poured out my heart, my soul and my thoughts, believing that God will help at least one person from the contents within.

How To Use This Devotional

Each day is broken down into four sections outlined as a quick bible study for you. First section is led with a scripture from the Old Testament. Second section are my personal thoughts and commentary on that scripture. Third section is an intimate prayer between you and God. Fourth section is your personal application to write down what the scripture meant to you and how you can apply it to your day. My best recommendation is to read this daily devotional at your own pace. Take time to process the material and allow God to speak to you through it. I pray that the Holy Spirit would guide you and direct you; that He would give you eyes to see, ears to hear and a heart to understand the things God wants to show you. Be blessed my friends and take this time to really draw near to our creator, the closer you get to Him, the clearer His voice becomes.

DAY ONE

"But they who wait on the Lord shall renew their strength; they shall mount up with wings like eagles; they shall run and not be weary; they shall walk and not faint."

Isaiah 40:31

Patience is key in all aspects of life. What I've found to be of the utmost importance in our walk with God is patience. We must understand that He sees far and beyond anything we can comprehend. I often get caught up in the flow of life and try to outrun God, but it never works in my favor. I have to constantly remind myself that God has a good and perfect calling for my life that far surpasses my wildest dreams. It's my job to wait for His nudging to pursue the things He wants me to pursue, with understanding that He is always on time and He never makes mistakes. All things will work for His glory and according to His timing. I may get tired, I may get weary, I may be exhausted but knowing that God is my source of strength keeps me moving forward. God says so in His words that He will give you rest, He will give you power, He will recharge your battery. He is good and faithful to His promises.

PRAYER

Heavenly Father, I ask that you help me to see that You are in full control. Help me see that the life, vision, dreams, and goals You set ahead of me far outweigh anything I can fathom. Thank You for Your guidance and leadership through Your Holy Spirit, amen.

NOTES

_____

_____

_____

_____

<u>MEANING</u>

What does today's scripture mean to you?

_____

_____

_____

_____

_____

_____

_____

_____

APPLICATION

How can you apply this to your day?

_____

_____

_____

_____

_____

_____

_____

_____

DAY TWO

"And God said, 'Let us make man in our image, according to our likeness;"

Genesis 1:26

The Bible says we are made in the image of God. How powerful is that? Growing up, I was always being teased by my outer appearance. Being bi-racial, I never knew who I fit in with. On top of that, I was an overweight kid, and for a lack of a better word, a dork. All my life I struggled with fitting in and went to extreme lengths to be accepted. I took drugs and drank alcohol to be popular; engaged in sexual acts at an early age to fill voids; expressed anger to feel more powerful; and got in trouble to be noticed. I did whatever I could to find my place. It wasn't until I gave my life to Christ when I understood that I am fearfully and wonderfully made, that I was handcrafted by God and made specifically for His purpose and that I am exactly who God made me to be. This is where I find my peace, my strength, and my confidence, knowing that God handcrafted me in my mother's womb for the purpose of bringing Him glory.

PRAYER

Lord, give me the peace and understanding to know that I am who we are because You made me so. I know You do not make mistakes and every little crease, crevice, grin, smile, and cork is a part of You because I have been made in Your image, in Jesus name, amen.

NOTES

_____

_____

_____

_____

MEANING

What does today's scripture mean to you?

_____

_____

_____

_____

_____

_____

_____

_____

<u>APPLICATION</u>

How can you apply this to your day?

_____

_____

_____

_____

_____

_____

_____

_____

_____

DAY THREE

"Do not fear, for I am with you; Do not anxiously look about you, for I am your God. I will strengthen you, surely I will help you, surely I will uphold you with My righteous right hand."

Isaiah 41:10

Fear, anxiety and worry all come from the enemy. God specifically instructs us to remember He is with us. He will help us; He will uphold us. Why do we struggle with this so often? In the middle of the storm it can be hard to see the brighter day ahead and when we are faced with these struggles, we find it hard to keep our eyes off the problem and on our savior. When we are dealing with these things, we must run to Him. We must retreat to comfort of the shelter He provides. It cannot be our last resort; it must be our first instinct and reaction. We have to remind the enemy of who our God is. I believe by getting into His presence through prayer and reading His word, we will be better equipped to fight the good fight and quicker to run to Him. God is the same today as He was yesterday and will be the same tomorrow. He is unmovable, unchanging and should be our first line of defense every single day. Hold tight to the promises of God and use them to reassure you and give you the comfort you need in the face of fear, anxiety, and worry.

PRAYER

Heavenly Father, I just want to thank you for being my source of peace and comfort. I pray that You would breathe life into me when I am faced with challenges of this world. Take away all fear, worry and anxiety and overshadow me with your presence and give me the reassurance of your promises. Equip me with the knowledge of who You are, thank you Lord God. Amen.

NOTES

_____

_____

_____

_____

<u>MEANING</u>

What does today's scripture mean to you?

_____

_____

_____

_____

_____

_____

_____

_____

APPLICATION

How can you apply this to your day?

_____

_____

_____

_____

_____

_____

_____

_____

_____

DAY FOUR

"The Lord will fight for you. All you have to do is keep still."

Exodus 14:14

Having the confidence that God is willing to fight our battles is encouraging. The Bible says all we have to do is be still. But how many of us do just that? I know God will fight, but when the battle is raging and I do not see Him moving, it is hard to hold my peace. We have the assurance that God will do as He says. He is faithful. He is good. He is constant. Sit in that for a moment. How can we better trust that God will come to our aid? My encouragement to you is, as the battle rages on, sit patiently with the understanding that God is never late, He is always on time and that timing is perfect.

PRAYER

Father God, I know in my heart that You are good and faithful. Help me to be more patient, give me the ability to stay by Your side and in presence as the woes of life mount against me. In You I put my hope, my faith, and my trust, in Jesus mighty name, amen.

NOTES

_____

_____

_____

_____

<u>MEANING</u>

What does today's scripture mean to you?

_____

_____

_____

_____

_____

_____

_____

_____

APPLICATION

How can you apply this to your day?

_____

_____

_____

_____

_____

_____

_____

_____

DAY FIVE

"I have hidden your word in my heart that I might not sin against you."

Psalm 119:11

Sin is a real thing, and it is the reason Jesus died for us. Our sin separated us from God and for us to have a relationship with Him, a sacrifice had to be made. Even after we are saved and accept Jesus Christ as our Savior, sin is still a problem. Sin comes in many forms because the enemy is sneaky, cunning and has a way of distracting us and using our weaknesses against us. In this scripture, God is giving us some basic instructions that could not be clearer. To fight sin, to stay blameless, to win the battle we must write the word of God on our hearts. How do we do that? First, we have to be in the word of God.

We have to have passion and love for His word. It's one thing to read His word, it is another thing to study it, meditate in it and gain knowledge from it. Second, we have to invite the Holy Spirit into our life to take the word we consume and write it on our hearts. When we are faced with situations that can lead to sin, the word should be a light for our feet, so we do not stumble. It gives us guidance, discernment and helps us makes decisions that are pleasing to God. We hide His word in our hearts by consuming it and allowing the Holy Spirit to bring it forth in compromising situations. Only through His power and strength can we overcome our sinful nature.

PRAYER

Lord, I need You. I cannot do it without You. I ask that You write Your word on the tablet of my heart so that when the enemy comes against me, I can stand on Your word and Your truth. I know that enemy flees at the name Jesus, so be my shield, be my sword and lead me into battle, in the mighty name of Jesus, amen.

NOTES

_____

_____

_____

_____

<u>MEANING</u>

What does today's scripture mean to you?

_____

_____

_____

_____

_____

_____

_____

_____

APPLICATION

How can you apply this to your day?

_____

_____

_____

_____

_____

_____

_____

_____

DAY SIX

"God is not a human, that He should lie, not a human being, that He should change His mind. Does He speak and then not act? Does He promise and not fulfill?"

Numbers 23:19

People will fail you repeatedly. Your family, your friends, your coworkers, your acquaintances, etc. All of them. It varies by degree and it is not always done to hurt you, but repeatedly we will have expectations that are not met by the ones we rely on. That is not the case with God. Ever! We do not always get what we want when we want it, but that doesn't reflect the character of God. That shows us that are alignment with His will is off. He is never changing, He is faithful, He follows through on His promises, He does not lie. All our hope, trust and faith should be firmly planted and grounded in Him and the promises He is made to us found in His word. Do not be scared to lay it all down at the foot of His throne. He will never fail you. Only God can breathe new life into your situations and bring you into a new season. We need to understand that it does not always look the way we envisioned it, nor does it line up with our expectations, but we can be sure that what He has in store for us is better than what we could plan out.

PRAYER

Lord, I know You are good and faithful and there is no wrong found in You. Give me the peace of knowing that I can firmly place my trust in You. I thank You for Your unchanging love and for giving me a firm foundation to build a life that brings You honor and glory, amen.

NOTES

_____

_____

_____

_____

__MEANING__

What does today's scripture mean to you?

_____

_____

_____

_____

_____

_____

_____

_____

_____

APPLICATION

How can you apply this to your day?

_____

_____

_____

_____

_____

_____

_____

_____

DAY SEVEN

"Love the LORD your God with all your heart and with all your soul and with all your strength."

Deuteronomy 6:5

How can we love God with all our heart, all our soul and all our strength? For me, I've been able to accomplish this by putting Him first in everything I do. It's not easy by any means because the pace of the world gets the best of me from time to time. I try to make a point to put God at the forefront of all I do, every decision I make, before the things of this world and distractions suffocate me and my attention. I've also found practicing gratitude and thankfulness keep me focused on His goodness and not on my problems. I know this is paramount in having a relationship with Him and feeling His presence. Knowing the lengths God went to have a relationship with me keeps my eyes fixed on Him and in a constant state of thankfulness. When the world gets loud, I tune in to the voice of the Father and remember to love Him more than anything else.

PRAYER

Heavenly Father, I want to take a moment to let you know I love You. You are sovereign, You are above all other things. Help me to love You with every ounce of my being. Thank You for Your love mercy and grace, in Jesus name I pray, amen.

NOTES

_____

_____

_____

_____

MEANING

What does today's scripture mean to you?

_____

_____

_____

_____

_____

_____

_____

_____

<u>APPLICATION</u>

How can you apply this to your day?

_____

_____

_____

_____

_____

_____

_____

_____

DAY EIGHT

"Have I not commanded you? Be strong and courageous. Do not be afraid; do not be discouraged, for the LORD your God will be with you wherever you go."

Joshua 1:9

No matter what we are facing or going through we have the assurance that God is always by our side. It doesn't always feel like that though. I've found over the years that if God doesn't feel near to me it is because I have wandered off, not Him. He is steadfast, He is unmovable, He is sturdy. I often remind myself that He is with me if I only look. What does that look like? For me I have to seek Him in His word. I use a devotional or I read books about His relationship with us. I also pray, in word and in spirit. I will set aside time to talk with

Him, hold a conversation, sometimes just cry out. And I will worship Him. I will throw on some music and sing His praises regardless of my outside circumstances. This gives me the courage and strength to know that He is with me and by my side through everything the world has to throw at me.

PRAYER

Lord, I want to say thank You for never leaving my side. For being a constant source of strength and courage. I ask that you teach me to look for You when I feel space, to search for You relentlessly until I am close. I love You and worship You for being who You say You are, in Jesus name, amen.

NOTES

_____

_____

_____

_____

<u>MEANING</u>

What does today's scripture mean to you?

_____

_____

_____

_____

_____

_____

_____

_____

APPLICATION

How can you apply this to your day?

_____

_____

_____

_____

_____

_____

_____

_____

DAY NINE

"Now fear the LORD and serve Him with all faithfulness."

Joshua 24:14

What does fear the Lord mean to you? For me, it means to have a deep reverence and respect for Him. To know His power, to understand His ways, to respect His authority and to be aware that He is sovereign. No one and nothing are above Him. This puts things in perspective for me. He is the source of everything. That is some serious power and even though it makes me feel small, I feel so special that He would consider having a relationship with me. This fear makes me want to get to know Him better, to serve Him, to be faithful to Him. This fear draws me closer as it is rare to have unlimited access and relationship to a power that is almighty. This fear is not meant to keep us away but to bring us in closer like a moth to the light.

PRAYER

Heavenly Father help me to know and understand You better. Create in me a healthy fear and respect for who You are and what You wish to do in my life. Help me to serve You in a manner that brings glory to Your name and that is faithful all the days of my life, amen.

NOTES

_____

_____

_____

_____

__MEANING__

What does today's scripture mean to you?

_____

_____

_____

_____

_____

_____

_____

_____

<u>APPLICATION</u>

How can you apply this to your day?

_____

_____

_____

_____

_____

_____

_____

_____

DAY TEN

"No one will be able to stand against you all the days of your life. As I was with Moses, so I will be with you; I will never leave you nor forsake you."

Joshua 1:5

If God is for us, then who can be against us? This promise is so bold and transformational it gives me the encouragement needed in any season of life. He says He will be with us all the days of our lives. Good, bad, happy, sad, in turmoil, grief, depression, addiction, sin; no matter what we are going through. Then to say no one will stand against us! Lord, we hear You. This is confirmation as a believer we need to sit in. Our God loves us. He gave His son to have this relationship with us. This verse should help you regain the power and confidence needed to face any storm in life. God is so good and faithful it blows my mind. God tells us to be bold, to stand in authority, our God is bigger and greater than any situation you can think of. When the enemy is telling you otherwise and trying to sneak in with fear, doubt, and worry, remind the enemy of this verse. No one will stand against because our Father God is by our side and will fight our battles for us. Hallelujah!

PRAYER

Heavenly Father, I just want to say thank You for Your promise to be by my side and to always be my source of strength and power. Give me the boldness and confidence to face the enemy head on knowing that You will always be with me and nothing will separate me from Your love in the mighty name of Jesus I pray, amen.

NOTES

_____

_____

_____

_____

__MEANING__

What does today's scripture mean to you?

_____

_____

_____

_____

_____

_____

_____

_____

APPLICATION

How can you apply this to your day?

_____

_____

_____

_____

_____

_____

_____

_____

DAY ELEVEN

"The LORD does not look at the things human beings look at. People look at the outward appearance, but the LORD looks at the heart."

1 Samuel 16:7

This verse brings me so much joy because before I was saved, I always thought of a Christian as looking a certain way. In my mind, there was a cookie cutter mold that all people had to adhere to in order to be an effective witness for Christ. It wasn't until God started using me that I realized God is not as concerned about our outer appearance as He is our heart. Yes, He wants us to follow Him and turn from sin, and it is not a free pass to do whatever you want, but it is confirmation that He doesn't look at us the way people look at us. The things that disqualify you with man does not always disqualify you with God. In fact, God uses the foolish things of this world, the people others count out, the folk's others see as a mess and use them in miraculous ways. God wants able bodies He can use as vessels for the Holy Spirit. They come in all shapes, sizes, colors and have different experiences, failures, backgrounds, and testimonies. You should never judge the vessels God is using for His glory. Look at the fruits of their life, are they clear? Can you see God moving? Although it is not up to us who God uses, we often get caught up worrying about how other Christians walk with God when the only journey we should be focusing on is our own. A good rule of thumb is to stay in your own lane, focus on your walk with God and encourage others along the way regardless of what they look like. We should not treat others like God loves them less than He loves us.

PRAYER

Thank you, Lord, for seeing past my outer appearance. I am thankful that You can use me as I am. Look at my heart Father God and help me to rid any judgement, arrogance or pride that keeps me from loving Your people. Fill me with Your grace and understanding and teach me to see others as You do, for what is on the inside and not what is on the outside, in Jesus name, amen.

NOTES

_____

_____

_____

_____

MEANING

What does today's scripture mean to you?

_____

_____

_____

_____

_____

_____

_____

_____

<u>APPLICATION</u>

How can you apply this to your day?

_____

_____

_____

_____

_____

_____

_____

_____

DAY TWELVE

*"And observe what the LORD your God
requires: Walk in obedience to Him, and
keep His decrees and commands, His
laws, and regulations, as written in the Law
of Moses. Do this so that you may prosper
in all you do and wherever you go."*

1 Kings 2:3

We all want to prosper in life. No one
wants to live a life filled with struggle,
stress, and anxiousness. Being a Christian
is not promised to be easy, it is not
promised that you will be rich or successful
either. In fact, it says that our riches are
stored in Heaven, the things of this world
will fade away and eventually be
destroyed. With that said, to prosper in my
mind means to be provided for, to have
enough, to be taken care of and God does

and will always do just that. This verse I believe can be misinterpreted and used for a gospel of prosperity. If you are obedient and follow His laws, you will get rich. I do not buy that. I do believe that if we are not walking according to His word that the good things in life can be withheld. That if we are on our own path verses God's path, we cannot tap into the good things God has set aside for us or we will miss the things of God. To prosper looks different for everyone. This is what I do know. Having a heart for the things of the Lord, obeying His word, and following Him faithfully will lead us all down different paths, however, we can rest assured that whatever it is and wherever He takes you, He will have His hand over your life and you'll be taken care of.

PRAYER

Lord God, I want to give You praise for always knowing my need and always supplying according to Your will. Help me to see the path You want me to travel because I know that is where I will find purpose, vison, and drive. Give me a heart that searches out the things You have laid out in front of me and help me to follow You in obedience, in Jesus name I pray, amen.

NOTES

_____

_____

_____

__MEANING__

What does today's scripture mean to you?

_____

_____

_____

_____

_____

_____

_____

_____

APPLICATION

How can you apply this to your day?

_____

_____

_____

_____

_____

_____

_____

_____

DAY THIRTEEN

"If my people, who are called by my name, will humble themselves and pray and seek my face and turn from their wicked ways, then I will hear from Heaven, and I will forgive their sin and will heal their land."

2 Chronicles 7:14

The world that we live in is a wreck. Disease, famine, war, death, violence, hatred, it is everywhere. You cannot turn on the television, open your phone or glance at a newspaper without seeing a new act of violence, sexual immorality, or wickedness in the headlines. How do we have victory in this area? This scripture speaks volumes about that. We need to repent, not just as a nation, but on a global scale. We have allowed evil to take over and are being bullied into silence as Christians. It takes an act of humility to say that we have been wrong, we have been weak, we have been blind, and we have ignored the word of God. We need revival and it starts with us. We have to start making a stand, no more hiding in the shadows, no more being ashamed of the name of Jesus, no more allowing the wicked to dominate without standing on our truth and saying something. It starts in our own personal sphere of influence whether that is your home, your community, your work, social media, school etc. We cannot allow the fear of being looked down on, losing our position and reputation, or people judging us because God is with us. He is our source of strength, power, courage, and boldness. He has given us authority and it is time we took it back. It starts with us!

PRAYER

Heavenly Father give me the words to speak, the course of action to take and the boldness to execute Your will for my life. Help me to take back the land that You have established. I need Your authority and power to make these moves and I invite Your Holy Spirit into my life to lead me and guide me in this modern-day revival, in Jesus name, amen.

NOTES

_____

_____

_____

_____

MEANING

What does today's scripture mean to you?

_____

_____

_____

_____

_____

_____

_____

_____

<u>APPLICATION</u>

How can you apply this to your day?

_____

_____

_____

_____

_____

_____

_____

_____

_____

DAY FOURTEEN

"Be still, and know that I am God; I will be exalted among the nations, I will be exalted in the earth."

Psalm 46:10

People often ask how do I hear the voice of God? For me, it comes when I am still. When I carve out time in my day, set aside all distractions and get quiet. The world is loud. We are surrounded by things fighting for our attention every second of every hour. How can we expect God to speak to us or for us to even hear His voice if we are constantly talking or filling the silent void with noise? To have a clear understanding of who God is, we have to pursue Him and many times that pursuit comes with stillness and silence. It is not always easy, and it takes work, but anything worth having takes work. To have a better understanding of God, a better relationship with God and the ability to hear His voice is priceless so take some time for Him daily. Clear up some space in your life and start making God a priority. For when He comes back, you will want to hear, "well done my good and faithful servant."

PRAYER

Father God help me to focus on You more. I know I need You and I know I need to make more time for You. I pray that You would close doors that are not from You, that You would tear away distractions that take my eyes off You. Guide me into a quiet place where I can hear Your voice and see Your face, in the name of Jesus, amen.

NOTES

_____

_____

_____

MEANING

What does today's scripture mean to you?

_____

_____

_____

_____

_____

_____

_____

_____

APPLICATION

How can you apply this to your day?

_____

_____

_____

_____

_____

_____

_____

_____

DAY FIFTEEN

"For you created my inmost being; you knit me together in my mother's womb."

Psalm 139:13

How amazing is that? We are hand crafted uniquely by God. We are intimately known by the creator of the universe. He looked at the world and thought it needed one of you. That's powerful! Why are we so hard on ourselves? Why do we compare ourselves to others knowing that God made us exactly how we are? This world tells us to how to behave, look and act a certain way. That message is to conform to the world's "normal." Be like everyone else. Do not have an original thought. Do what's trending. God says otherwise. Do not conform to this world. Be uniquely you. You are fearfully and wonderfully made.

You are a one of one, limited edition, exclusive version of you. You are exactly who God made you to be. You have a special set of skills and attributes that He wants you to use to bring glory to His name. When we follow others or try to be someone we are not designed to be, we are dulling our own light. We are not walking in the fullness God has called us to. We have to find that place where we love who we are in Christ, we stand bold in our appearance, we walk tall as children of God and are not ashamed of who God made us to be. We are made in His image.

PRAYER

Lord God, I ask that You breathe Your life into me and give me the courage to be who You made me to be. I love You and want to take this moment to give You praise, honor and glory. I know that every knee shall bow, and every tongue shall confess that You are Lord. I want to establish Your presence and authority in my life by saying thank you Jesus. Amen.

NOTES

_____

_____

_____

_____

<u>MEANING</u>

What does today's scripture mean to you?

_____

_____

_____

_____

_____

_____

_____

_____

APPLICATION

How can you apply this to your day?

_____

_____

_____

_____

_____

_____

_____

_____

DAY SIXTEEN

"I know that my redeemer lives, and that in the end he will stand on the earth."

Job 19:25

God is real. We have this hope and faith that not everyone believes or understands. Many people call Christians foolish, criticize us, make fun of us, and tease us. I often say that if the world did not like Jesus then people are not going to like us. The thing is that not everyone is called. Not everyone makes Heaven their home. We have been chosen, hand crafted and set aside. We are Gods people and we were made for times like these. He is coming back to judge. He is coming back for His people. Until then, we try our absolute best to live a life that is pleasing to Him and that honors Him. No one knows the day, but rest assured He is coming. This should give you a sense of urgency. Ask God to forgive you for your secret sins and repent from them. Give those evil thoughts, additions or guilt you are struggling with to God so you can find the strength to end them. Tell the people in your life about God who do not know Him or do not want to believe in Him. It is time to get your affairs in order. There is no time to waste. Our Savior has called us to do His mighty work and His mighty work is what we will do.

PRAYER

Lord, I know that You live. I invite Your Holy Spirit into my life to help me be who You have called me to be. Help me to be faithful witnesses to the glory You've bestowed upon me. I thank You for allowing me to partake in the development of Your kingdom. Give me the sense of urgency and the knowledge of how important it is to do Your bidding before You come back for Your people. I pray this in the power of Your name, amen.

NOTES

_____

_____

_____

<u>MEANING</u>

What does today's scripture mean to you?

_____

_____

_____

_____

_____

_____

_____

_____

APPLICATION

How can you apply this to your day?

_____

_____

_____

_____

_____

_____

_____

_____

DAY SEVENTEEN

"The Spirit of God has made me; the breath of the Almighty gives me life."

Job 33:4

We are nothing without God. I lived a lot of life separate from His presence and let me tell you, life had no meaning, no purpose, and no direction. We are in a physical body that is growing older and getting closer to death every day, but our spirits are the breath of God. Our sole purpose is to do His work, to follow His plan and to act out His will. Nothing else! We have to remember that this life is not about us. It is so much bigger. We can easily get wrapped up in the things of this world which cause us to get distracted and off track. This is a reminder that there is no life without His breath. The ultimate show of love and respect is to sacrifice our earthly lives to Him by living according to His plan. To give Him praise, to bring Him glory, to have relationship with Him, our creator, the orchestrator of the universe.

PRAYER

Father God fill me with Your Holy Spirit. Allow me to be an empty vessel for Your precious breath. Give me the strength and power to do Your work. Help me to be sensitive to the calling you have on my life and give me the courage to stand boldly on Your truths while I share with the world the love, mercy, and grace You provide, amen.

NOTES

_____

_____

_____

_____

MEANING

What does today's scripture mean to you?

_____

_____

_____

_____

_____

_____

_____

_____

APPLICATION

How can you apply this to your day?

_____

_____

_____

_____

_____

_____

_____

_____

_____

DAY EIGHTEEN

*"He performs wonders that cannot be
fathomed, miracles that cannot be
counted."*

Job 9:10

Time and time again I have watched the
hands of God move. He makes miracles
out of messes. He can make praise out of
pain. He will turn victims into victors. We
are talking about the creator of the
universe who has unlimited resources and
power indescribable. No situation is too
dire, no obstacle too big or issue too
complex. The things that are impossible
with man are always possible with God. It
can be mind-blowing to think how He
works. God is always a million steps ahead
of what we are dealing with and has a
solution to every problem. The issue is that

many times we try to put God in a box and only think He can move with the same limitations we are bound by. We have to take solace and find peace in the fact that He will always work things out for the good of those who love Him. So, when the world has your back against the wall and there doesn't seem like there is a way out, draw near to hear, be still, wait and know that He is God, and He will make a way.

PRAYER

Heavenly Father, I know You are almighty, and Your power is unmatched. Help me to find peace and understanding as You rise up against any situation that looks to distract me. I know that You are good and faithful and that You love Your people, help me to find rest in the glory of Your strength, amen.

NOTES

_____

_____

_____

_____

__MEANING__

What does today's scripture mean to you?

_____

_____

_____

_____

_____

_____

_____

_____

APPLICATION

How can you apply this to your day?

_____

_____

_____

_____

_____

_____

_____

_____

DAY NINETEEN

"I know that you can do all things; no purpose of yours can be thwarted."

Job 42:2

God can take things made by evil and make them out for His glory and purpose. No weapon formed against us will prosper if we surrender our will to our Heavenly Father. His purpose for your life outweighs and surpasses anything you can think of. Nothing is too much for our God. I often remind myself that He is never caught off guard. He always knows what is around the corner. Those life situations that blindsides us out of nowhere, God saw coming far in advance and already has a solution to it. That is why it is important for us to stay close to Him. The vision God has for your life is written on your heart.

We know what it is He wants us to do but because it doesn't line up with what we want, we quench the Holy Spirit, meaning we drown out that little voice and ignore it. We must be mindful that His purpose is going be done no matter how much we fight it. God has a way of taking us through the same lesson over and over until we get it right. So, when you see a pattern of something God is taking you through, it is important to slow down, draw near to Him and ask Him what it is He's trying to show you. What can you learn? Where is He leading you? How can you grow? With His guidance you can make it through and step into the next season He has waiting for you.

PRAYER

God in Heaven, I know that with You I can do all things. Help me to lay down my life, my goals, my dreams, and my visions at the foot of Your throne and give me the direction and leadership I so desperately need. Give me Your Holy Spirit to help me navigate the ups and downs of life and teach me to live that is obedient to Your calling, amen.

NOTES

_____

_____

_____

<u>MEANING</u>

What does today's scripture mean to you?

_____

_____

_____

_____

_____

_____

_____

_____

<u>APPLICATION</u>

How can you apply this to your day?

_____

_____

_____

_____

_____

_____

_____

_____

DAY TWENTY

"For if you remain silent at this time, relief and deliverance for the Jews will arise from another place, but you and your father's family will perish. And who knows but that you have come to royal position for such a time as this?"

Esther 4:14

Esther, a Jew, was placed in a position of power once she married the King. This verse is what Ester's uncle said to her. That there is a divine purpose as to why she was placed in a position to speak to the King on behalf of the Jews to stop a mass execution of their entire race. At first, she was hesitant and questioned her duty, but Ester did what God had put her in that position for. We all have a calling and destiny in the will of God. It is not always clear and a lot of the time we are following Him trying to make sense of the madness. What I have learned is with or without us, Gods will is going to be done. He wants to use us and has designed us for a specific purpose, but if we allow sin and our own free will to distract us, God will use the next available person to complete His good and perfect will. He can use our failures, mistakes, and struggles to teach us, to help us grow and put us in a position to bring glory to His name. Therefore, when the time comes to testify and use those experiences, we have to be ready. It is important to remain close to God, to walk with Him, rid your life of the things that separate you from Him so you can hear His voice and the nudging's from the Holy Spirit.

PRAYER

Father God help me to listen to Your voice. Give me the wisdom to know that everything I have, everywhere I go, everything I do and say is for Your divine purpose. Give me eyes to see Your will and teach me to be bold and courageous in those situations that do not always make sense but are clearly put in front of me to execute what You have planned out, in Jesus name, amen.

NOTES

_____

_____

_____

_____

MEANING

What does today's scripture mean to you?

_____

_____

_____

_____

_____

_____

_____

_____

APPLICATION

How can you apply this to your day?

_____

_____

_____

_____

_____

_____

_____

_____

DAY TWENTY-ONE

"Give me wisdom and knowledge, that I may lead this people, for who is able to govern this great people of yours?"

2 Chronicles 1:10

Of all the things Solomon could have asked for, this is what he wanted. Wisdom and knowledge. Why? How do we find wisdom and knowledge? It's found in understanding who God is and His character. It's found in His word. It's found in His presence. It's found in a right relationship with Him. These two things that Solomon asked for are available to us if we ask and we seek. Too many of us are not willing to do the work. We will spend hours a day scrolling and consuming social media but will not take the time to consume the word of God. Then wonder why we cannot feel or hear Him. It is imperative that we take the time to relentlessly search for His presence. Pray daily asking the Holy Spirit into your life to give you wisdom and knowledge and to reveal to you the truths of the word of God. Pray for Him to breathe life into your relationship with him. If you want to make an impact on others, if you want to have an on-fire relationship with God, if you want to lead His people and help them find our Savior, it starts with wisdom and knowledge, and it can only be found when you start to look.

PRAYER

God in Heaven let my heart sing to You because You are good and faithful. Fill my inner most being with Your knowledge and wisdom. Help me to seek You with the same vigor as I do the things of this world. I love You and pray You would awake that fire deep within my soul for the things You have set aside for Your people, in the name of Jesus I pray, amen.

NOTES

_____

_____

_____

_____

<u>MEANING</u>

What does today's scripture mean to you?

_____

_____

_____

_____

_____

_____

_____

_____

<u>APPLICATION</u>

How can you apply this to your day?

_____

_____

_____

_____

_____

_____

_____

_____

DAY TWENTY-TWO

*"The law of the LORD is perfect, refreshing
the soul. The statutes of the LORD are
trustworthy, making wise the simple."*

Psalm 19:7

God doesn't make mistakes. You are right
where you are supposed to be at this very
moment in time. Every choice, every
decision and every action has led you to
this time and space. God wants to use you
where you are at. There are people in your
life that need to hear about Jesus. There is
work to be done. We have to stop wishing
for another life, or waiting for a big break,
or our situation to change. God has you
there for a reason and if you can take your
eyes off your situation and put them on our
savior, His purpose will be revealed to you.
If you knock, He will answer, if you ask,

you will receive in accordance to His will. If you are asking and not receiving, that does not mean God doesn't hear you, it may be that what you are asking for is not a part of His will. He is perfect! If you want guidance in your situation and you want knowledge on how to handle things in your life, it is found in the unchanging word of God. When we set our eyes on Him and find our purpose in the season, He has us in, He begins to perform His miracles. So, no matter where you are in life, whether you are living the dream or working on it, make serving God your priority and watch Him breathe new life into your situation.

PRAYER

Heavenly Father, I want to thank You for Your endless love, mercy, and grace. Thank You for Your willingness to use me as I am. Help me to live a life that is pleasing to You and set Your purpose for me in front of my eyes so that I can do Your will, in Jesus name I pray, amen.

NOTES

_____

_____

_____

_____

<u>MEANING</u>

What does today's scripture mean to you?

_____

_____

_____

_____

_____

_____

_____

_____

<u>APPLICATION</u>

How can you apply this to your day?

_____

_____

_____

_____

_____

_____

_____

_____

DAY TWENTY-THREE

"Whoever dwells in the shelter of the Most High will rest in the shadow of the Almighty."

Psalm 91:1

God is our shelter. He is our refuge. He is our strong tower. If you want real, true, and authentic rest it has to be found in Him. Have you ever gone on vacation, and needed a vacation when you get back? We see rest differently than God. After creating the world, He took a rest day. Many times, our rest consists of doing things that we are told are healing actions, but more times than not, they are not. I would encourage you to take a real rest day. Not one you clutter up with things on your to do lists and little projects that have been piling up. A day to retreat in God. If you genuinely want to be refreshed, renewed, and revitalized, you have to make Him your shelter. What that looks like for me is shutting off my phone, turning off the television, finding a nice spot in a quiet corner of the house and just being still. I might pray, I might just listen. But I cut out all distractions and get into His presence. A feeling of peace, understanding and clarity is usually followed by these moments. How often do you take time like this? If you want the rest you desperately need, I encourage you to practice this at least a couple times a week. If you can do this daily, even better. Take time for you and the Lord and get into His presence regularly. Watch how your relationship with Him improves and how more at peace and rested you feel.

PRAYER

Father God, You are my shelter and my place of rest. I ask that You overshadow and envelop me in Your protection. I need You Lord and pray that You would send Your Holy Spirit into my life to direct me, lead me and guide me. I long to be closer to You. I praise You from the depths of my heart; glory, honor and power be to You and You alone, in Jesus name, amen.

NOTES

_____

_____

_____

_____

__MEANING__

What does today's scripture mean to you?

_____

_____

_____

_____

_____

_____

_____

_____

APPLICATION

How can you apply this to your day?

_____

_____

_____

_____

_____

_____

_____

_____

_____

DAY TWENTY-FOUR

"The Lord bless you and keep you; The Lord make His face shine upon you and be gracious to you; The Lord lift up His countenance upon you and give you peace."

Numbers 6:24-26

Regardless of what is happening in my life, I can see God doing this in every season. It is either blatant and clear, or it may feel unbelievable, but the fact is if you are alive and breathing you are blessed. Life is never promised to be easy but each day we get to experience is a blessing. Gods face shines down on us even in the middle of a storm. His grace is extended every second of every day. His peace and comfort are always available. It is up to us as believers to seek that out and find it. It may not always easy, but we must remember that God doesn't change. He is never wrong; He does not make mistakes. The things we go through have a purpose and if we slow down, take the time to worship Him and seek His presence, we can unravel the things He wants us to see and will help us find purpose in the pain.

PRAYER

Heavenly Father. I ask that You would help me see the purpose in the pain. Help me to search out and find all the love, mercy, and grace You pour out onto me, even when it doesn't seem like it. I know You want the best for Your people, so I lay down my struggles and issues at the foot of Your throne. I ask that You would breath Your breathe into my situations. Amen.

NOTES

_____

_____

_____

<u>MEANING</u>

What does today's scripture mean to you?

_____

_____

_____

_____

_____

_____

_____

_____

__APPLICATION__

How can you apply this to your day?

_____

_____

_____

_____

_____

_____

_____

_____

DAY TWENTY-FIVE

"Even though I walk through the darkest valley, I will fear no evil, for you are with me; your rod and your staff, they comfort me."

Psalm 23:4

When I hear this verse, I often think to myself how it is easier said than done. The valley is dark. The valley can be scary. The valley is filled with the unknown and evil. It cannot be that simple. Or is it? I tend to complicate things from time to time. The Bible tells us to have childlike faith but during the storm even Peter, one of Jesus's disciples, struggled with doubt. He trusted Jesus enough to step out on the water but then looked at the storm and lost his faith. We tend to do the same thing. We will set off into the valley with full intentions on keeping our faith strong, leaning into God, but when it starts to get heavy, we shrink and forget God is with us. His rod and staff comfort us. His presence comforts us. This is a solid reminder that when the world seems too big and our problems keep getting bigger, He is with us always. Nothing is too big, no evil too powerful, no mountain too large because we serve the God of possibility. He is the way maker. He is our refuge. He is our strength. He is our provider. In Him we lack no provision. We have to keep this written on our heart and at the forefront of our memory.

PRAYER

Lord God, creator of all, I am humbled by Your power and strength. I look to You for my protection, I look to You as my source of provision, my eyes are fixed on You as I navigate this dark and treacherous world. The enemy has set snares and traps before me, but God I know that You are my deliverer and in You I put my trust, in the name of Jesus I pray, amen.

NOTES

_____

_____

_____

_____

MEANING

What does today's scripture mean to you?

_____

_____

_____

_____

_____

_____

_____

<u>APPLICATION</u>

How can you apply this to your day?

_____

_____

_____

_____

_____

_____

_____

_____

DAY TWENTY-SIX

"Trust in the LORD with all your heart and lean not on your own understanding"

Proverbs 3:5

My own understanding can be suspect and a complete liability sometimes. When I think I know, I have absolutely no idea. God is so patient with me as I try to trust in Him, but I can be so easily distracted or led off course. I've found the only way to truly trust in Him with all my heart, and not on my own understanding, is to submerge myself in His word and in His presence. I must be quiet and still. By doing this, I can better tune into His calling and direction for my life. So many people search for this feeling from God yet are so quick to fill their silence with distractions. Sermons, podcasts, and worship music are great emotional connectors to our Father, however, to trust and understand God, you have to shut everything down and clear space in your heart to fill His word in.

PRAYER

Father God, I ask that You lead me to a quiet place where I can have an intimate relationship with You. I so desperately want to know Your heart and will for my life. I surrender my own narrow view and understanding and pray that You would breathe new life into my walk with You, amen.

NOTES

_____

_____

_____

_____

__MEANING__

What does today's scripture mean to you?

_____

_____

_____

_____

_____

_____

_____

_____

<u>APPLICATION</u>

How can you apply this to your day?

_____

_____

_____

_____

_____

_____

_____

_____

DAY TWENTY-SEVEN

"The fear of the LORD is the beginning of knowledge, but fools despise wisdom and instruction."

Proverbs 1:7

I have walked the road of a fool. I've ignored instruction, I have hated discipline, I never would seek wisdom. I would go about my life as I saw fit. Chasing after accolades and achievements. Never stopping to check in with or acknowledge God. I can look back at this time in my life and I feel so much pain for who I was. I am scared to go back to that place. I did not realize how lost I was when I was there and that is the part that scares me. I have to constantly check my heart. I have to constantly be in His presence. I have to constantly lean into Him and ask if I am where I am supposed to be. Outside of Gods will is not a good place. Its filled with hurt, pain, regret, turmoil, frustration, and hardship. As a believer who has experienced the goodness of God, I do not want to spend one moment outside of Him. A fear I have is to be away from God, to not be aligned with where He wants me, to not have relationship with Him. Knowing who I was and who I've become, I believe we can learn to develop a healthy fear of the Lord that will lead us to being a good and faithful servant.

PRAYER

God in Heaven, I enter Your presence by the blood of Jesus. I ask that You instill a healthy fear and reverence in me for who You are. Lead me along the path You have laid out before me. Help me to stick to Your commands and to live a life that is pleasing to You. I ask for Your wisdom, knowledge and understanding and know that it comes with a heavy price of discipline and sacrifice. My hope, faith and trust are in You, amen.

NOTES

_____

_____

_____

_____

__MEANING__

What does today's scripture mean to you?

_____

_____

_____

_____

_____

_____

_____

_____

<u>APPLICATION</u>

How can you apply this to your day?

_____

_____

_____

_____

_____

_____

_____

_____

_____

DAY TWENTY-EIGHT

"Above all else, guard your heart, for everything you do flows from it."

Proverbs 4:23

Are you guarding your heart? What do you allow into it? Make no mistake, the music, shows, books and social media you consume sink down into your inner most being and take root in your heart. There is no room or place for these things. You cannot play with fire and not be burned. If everything you consume flows out from your heart, can you analyze your life and find areas you need to improve in? Lust? Foul Speech? Anger? Jealousy? Just to name a few. As Christians, we have to set ourselves aside and be mindful of the things we allow in our mind, body, and soul. It is easy to justify and make excuses for why it is acceptable, but we have been called to a higher purpose. There is no living one foot in and foot out. We cannot be a lukewarm Christian or else God will spit us out of His mouth. It's time to break your old habits that flow from your heart and let God set you free from those chains of bondage.

PRAYER

Heavenly Father help me to guard my hearts. Lord I need you to tear down any strongholds or chains of bondage that keep me stuck. Give me the courage and boldness to stand on your truth and move forward into the goodness that you have set aside for me, in the mighty name of Jesus I pray, amen.

NOTES

_____

_____

_____

_____

MEANING

What does today's scripture mean to you?

_____

_____

_____

_____

_____

_____

_____

_____

APPLICATION

How can you apply this to your day?

_____

_____

_____

_____

_____

_____

_____

_____

DAY TWENTY-NINE

"As iron sharpens iron, so one person sharpens another."

Proverbs 27:17

This is a pivotal verse that has so much wisdom and knowledge. It has to be employed into our daily life if we want to truly develop as Christians. We were made for relationships. First with God, then with other believers. I cannot put a number to how many instances a timely word from a brother or sister in Christ pulled me from the pit of despair. There have been times where I was wrong in my behavior or action, and their gentle correction brought me to reality. We need those relationships who help sharpen our souls with the body of Christ. People have said they stopped seeking God because a church or a Christian put a bad taste in their mouth. These are excuses to not build a relationship with God. If you go to a barber and get a bad haircut you do not cancel all barbers for the rest of your life. You find another one. And if that one doesn't work; you keep going until you find one that works for you. God has a body of believers for you. You can find faithful believers by joining a bible study or a connect group either at a church near you or online. If you want to experience the fullness of what God has promised us, a big part of it is in relationships with other believers. As you grow stronger in your walk with God, you become a vessel for others you will have to be able and willing to sharpen others when the time comes, just as your brothers and sister in Christ help sharpen you. Equally filling your cup and other cups are important. We stay sharp by being in the word of God, living a life that is pleasing to Him and constantly being in his presence.

PRAYER

Father God help me to be a blessing to others by keeping me sharp. Lord keep me in Your presence. My eyes are fixed on You. I pray for opportunity to share Your word, to minister to the lost and to add value to Your body as an integral part what You are doing. Thank You for choosing me to be a part of Your kingdom, in Jesus name, amen.

NOTES

_____

_____

_____

__MEANING__

What does today's scripture mean to you?

_____

_____

_____

_____

_____

_____

_____

_____

<u>APPLICATION</u>

How can you apply this to your day?

_____

_____

_____

_____

_____

_____

_____

_____

DAY THIRTY

"A cheerful heart is good medicine, but a crushed spirit dries up the bones."

Proverbs 17:22

As believers, as Christians, as children of the Most High God, we have a lot to be thankful for. Love, mercy, grace, forgiveness of our sins, multiple chances, salvation, and just life in general. We have been chosen, set aside, appointed, and handpicked. We are blessed! It's easy to get lost in the everyday grind and allow our outer circumstances to overwhelm us. But if you are alive and reading this, you are blessed beyond measure. We have to make practice of putting things in perspective. You may not be where you want to be, you may not have the things you want, you may not be satisfied with the hand life dealt you, but Gods purpose for your life is so much bigger than all of that. Lay all your wants and needs at the foot of His throne and reflect on the glory that awaits you. Doing this is my source of joy. Anytime you feel the weight of the world crushing your bones, reflect on the goodness of God, His character and who He is. Everything in this world pales in comparison to His glory.

PRAYER

God in Heaven help me to keep the thought of who You are at the forefront of my mind. Help me to remember Your promises and to remember who You say I am in You. My hope, my faith and my trust are firmly placed in You. I love You lord; I thank You and I praise You. Help me to find my truest form of joy in all that You do, in Jesus name, amen.

NOTES

_____

_____

_____

_____

__MEANING__

What does today's scripture mean to you?

_____

_____

_____

_____

_____

_____

_____

_____

APPLICATION

How can you apply this to your day?

_____

_____

_____

_____

_____

_____

_____

_____

DAY THIRTY-ONE

"There is a time for everything, and a season for every activity under the Heavens."

Ecclesiastes 3:1

There are good times and there are bad. Happy and sad. Life is filled with ups and down, highs and lows, peaks and valleys, rock bottoms and mountaintops. That is part of the journey. No one is immune to the journey of life. It all varies by degree, but one thing we can be sure of is that life is constantly changing like the seasons. The promise that I cling to is God is with us through it all. He knows everything we are going through, He knows our needs, He knows our worries, He knows our cares, He knows our goals, He knows our passions, He knows our dreams. He knows it all! We have to remember that He wants what is best for us. He doesn't operate by what we want, He goes by what we need, and He is faithful to see to it that we always have it. He is a loving and caring God who provides. We have to believe that each season has a purpose. To grow us, to refine us, to teach us, to humble us, to remind us and more. We have to search for the meaning in each season and it is revealed in the mighty presence of our Heavenly Father. A lot of the time our first inclination when we do not get what we want is to throw a tantrum, get upset with God, take things into our own hands but we have to stay mindful that He is in control and everything done has a divine purpose.

PRAYER

Heavenly Father keep me mindful of Your good and faithful will. Teach me to find rest in You and understanding in knowing that Your divine plan far outweighs anything I can fathom. I invite You Holy Spirit into my heart to lead me, guide me and direct me through all the seasons of life, in the name of Jesus I pray, amen.

NOTES

_____

_____

_____

_____

<u>MEANING</u>

What does today's scripture mean to you?

_____

_____

_____

_____

_____

_____

_____

_____

APPLICATION

How can you apply this to your day?

_____

_____

_____

_____

_____

_____

_____

_____

Made in the USA
Columbia, SC
24 February 2022

56791893R00089